A Little PDA Goes a Long Way

A Little PDA Goes a Long Way:
Strategies for Content Literacy

Pamela T. Bell

authorHOUSE®

AuthorHouse™ LLC
1663 Liberty Drive
Bloomington, IN 47403
www.authorhouse.com
Phone: 1-800-839-8640

Published by AuthorHouse   01/30/2014

ISBN: 978-1-4918-5878-3 (sc)
ISBN: 978-1-4918-5877-6 (e)

Library of Congress Control Number: 2014901805

http://en.wikipedia.org/wiki/File:Abraham_Lincoln_November_1863.jpg

http://en.wikipedia.org/wiki/File:Robert_Edward_Lee.jpg

http://en.wikipedia.org/wiki/File:Ulysses_Grant_1870-1880.jpg

http://en.wikipedia.org/wiki/File:Stonewall_Jackson.jpg

Contents

PRE-READING STRATEGIES

DURING READING STRATEGIES

AFTER READING STRATEGIES

A Little PDA Goes a Long Way.....

    When I first began researching content literacy strategies over a decade ago, I was surprised to find that few resources were available to improve comprehension in the content areas. I then knew there was a gap in educational strategies available to educators. Most content area teachers do not perceive themselves as "reading teachers," when in essence, we are all reading teachers. When reading comprehension does not occur, the teacher must be able to step in and assist students.   The old "assign and tell" method of instruction simply does not work with the students we currently serve.

    With that thought in mind, I began to work on strategies that can be used throughout the reading process at any grade level. Hence, the title- PDA: **p**re-reading, **d**uring reading, and **a**fter reading strategies. Over the years I have collected these strategies, while encouraging my elementary and secondary education student teachers at Gordon State College to do the same. What follows is a collection of these content area reading strategies. A description of the strategy is given, along with a template that may be used in the classroom. Also included for many of the strategies are actual student samples from the classroom.

Pre-reading

Methods to: Assess prior knowledge

                Increase knowledge on subject

                Introduce vocabulary

                Create reader interest

                Make predictions

                Set the stage before reading

During reading

Methods to: Guide interaction with the text

Develop vocabulary knowledge

Ensure that students comprehend before moving on

After reading

Methods to: Review major concepts

Review predictions

Review vocabulary

Ensure comprehension

I hope that you find these strategies helpful for your students and that you will soon see that "A Little PDA Goes a Long Way."

Pre-reading Strategies

STRATEGY 1

Do I Know These Words?

When students encounter unfamiliar vocabulary in a passage, their comprehension is severely affected. This pre-reading activity provides teachers with the opportunity to assess students' prior knowledge of the vocabulary words and increase that knowledge before reading. Students tire of the "look it up in the dictionary" approach, and this activity provides an engaging alternative.

<u>Suggestions for use</u>:

This activity is used on both an individual and group basis. The teacher should give each student a copy of the "Do I Know These Words" handout. A list of the vocabulary words will be listed at the bottom of the sheet. Students should be given around five to ten minutes to complete the worksheet. Students will put the words in the correct column based on their knowledge of the words. After students complete the worksheets, the teacher should use whole group discussion to cover each word and its meaning.

Do I know these words?

NOPE. NEVER SEEN IT!	HAVE SEEN OR HEARD THE WORD BUT I DON'T KNOW WHAT IT MEANS!	I THINK I MAY KNOW WHAT IT MEANS!	YES! YES! YES! I KNOW THIS WORD!

Word list:

STRATEGY 2

Connection Cards

Connection cards can be used to create a study guide for the vocabulary words that students are covering. The purpose of these cards is for the student to make a personal connection with each vocabulary word. This strategy is an improvement on the normal "write the definition and use it in a sentence" vocabulary exercise. Connection cards allow students to use their creativity and put a personal stamp on each word.

Suggestions for Use:

These cards should be completed individually so that the student may make his own personal connection with each word. A note card should be divided into four equal sections: in the first section, the word is listed; in the second section students will write their definition of the word (which should have been discussed previously with the students). The third section is used for the student to draw some representation, whether it is a symbol or picture, of the word. Finally, the last section can be used for different purposes: antonyms, synonyms, sentences, etc. The teacher will decide the use of the fourth section.

Even though students complete their cards individually, they should share cards with the class. Students benefit from hearing others' personal connections with the words and may choose to add something else to their existing picture or symbol.

CONNECTION CARDS

ultimatum	demand that is backed up with a threat
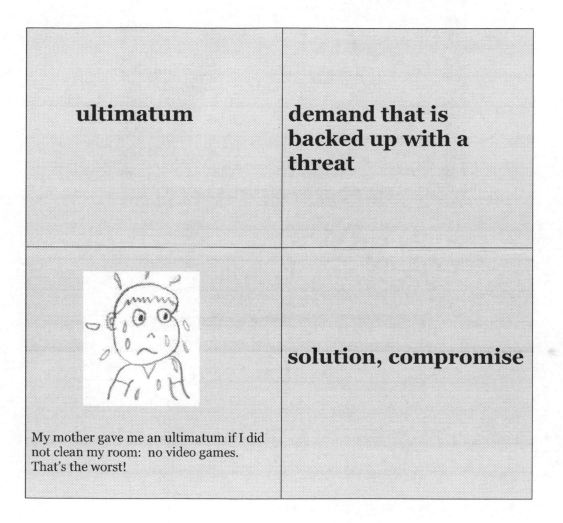 My mother gave me an ultimatum if I did not clean my room: no video games. That's the worst!	solution, compromise

Sample Third and Fourth Grade Connection Cards

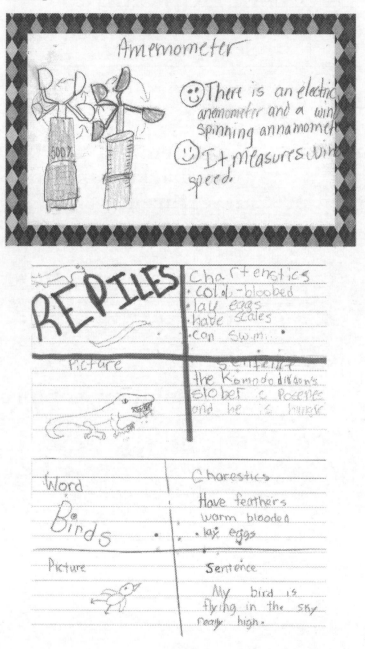

STRATEGY 3

Vocabulary Circle

Vocabulary circle is a visual organizer that helps students understand key words and concepts. The circle is divided into four or more equal sections to hold words or symbols that are connected by a common relationship. They create a visual reference for how the concepts are related and can be used effectively in all subject areas.

<u>Suggested Use:</u>

To construct a vocabulary circle, use the pattern provided or divide a circle into four (or more) sections. In each section write a word or phrase related to the topic or word. Circles may be used in three ways:

1. All of the words in the circle are related and the students must tell how they are related.
2. All of the words in the circle are related except one. The student must identify the unrelated word and explain how the other words are related.
3. One or more of the sections is left blank. Students must fill in the blank sections with words that are related to the other words in the circle and explain why they chose those words.

VOCABULARY CIRCLE PATTERN

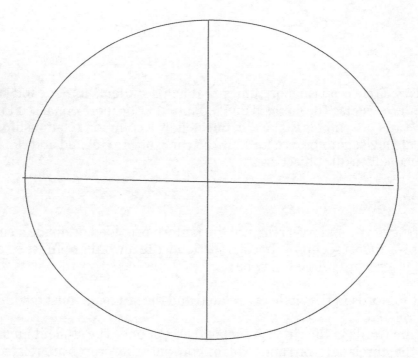

SAMPLE USES OF VOCABULARY CIRCLE

Which word does not belong? Shade the word that does not belong.

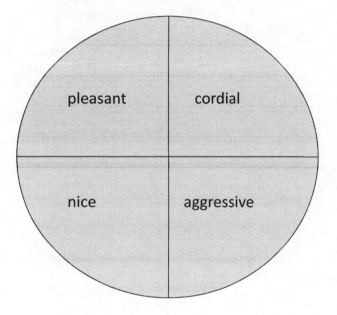

What is the vocabulary word that is a synonym to these words? Write it in the space.

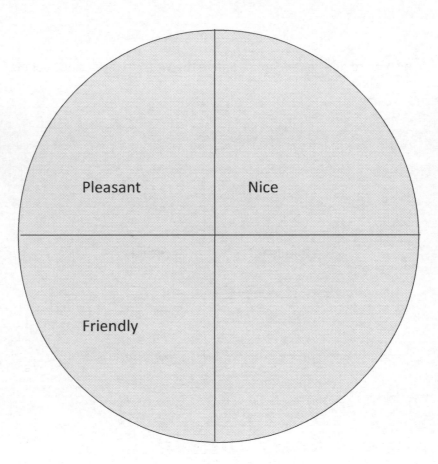

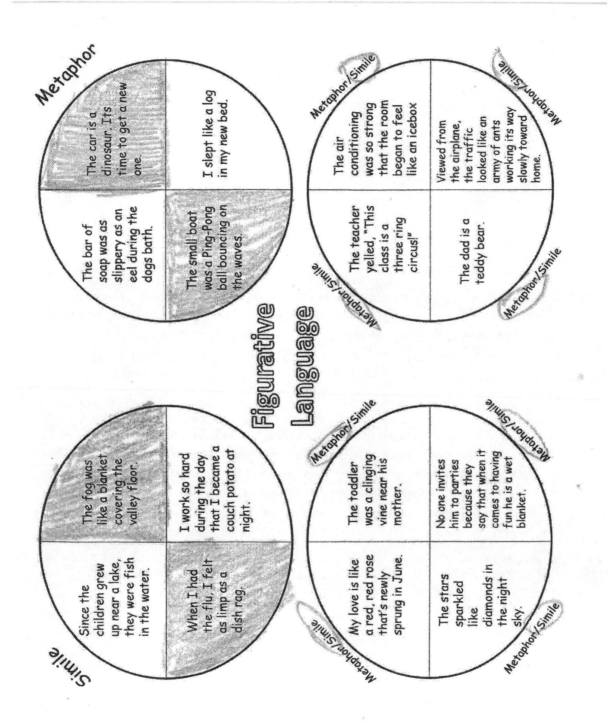

Figurative Language

Metaphor

The car is a dinosaur. Its time to get a new one.

I slept like a log in my new bed.

The bar of soap was as slippery as an eel during the dogs bath.

The small boat was a Ping-Pong ball bouncing on the waves.

Metaphor/Simile

The air conditioning was so strong that the room began to feel like an icebox

Viewed from the airplane, the traffic looked like an army of ants working its way slowly toward home.

Metaphor/Simile

The teacher yelled, "This class is a three ring circus!"

The dad is a teddy bear.

Metaphor/Simile

Simile

The fog was like a blanket covering the valley floor.

I work so hard during the day that I became a couch potato at night.

Since the children grew up near a lake, they were fish in the water.

When I had the flu, I felt as limp as a dish rag.

Metaphor/Simile

The toddler was a clinging vine near his mother.

No one invites him to parties because they say that when it comes to having fun he is a wet blanket.

Metaphor/Simile

My love is like a red, red rose that's newly sprung in June.

The stars sparkled like diamonds in the night sky.

Metaphor/Simile

13

STRATEGY 4

Map This Word

Word maps are diagrams that can be teacher or student created. They can help introduce new vocabulary, but more importantly, allow students to see the relationships and connections between words. These maps can be used in all subject areas and can also be completed as a during reading or after reading strategy.

<u>Suggested Use:</u>

This activity can be done individually or with a small group. However, the important aspect of this activity is not how the map is completed. The important part is making sure the maps are reviewed as a whole group. The teacher should make sure to review the correct answers on a master map with the class and elaborate on the relationships that are made within the map.

MAP THIS WORD

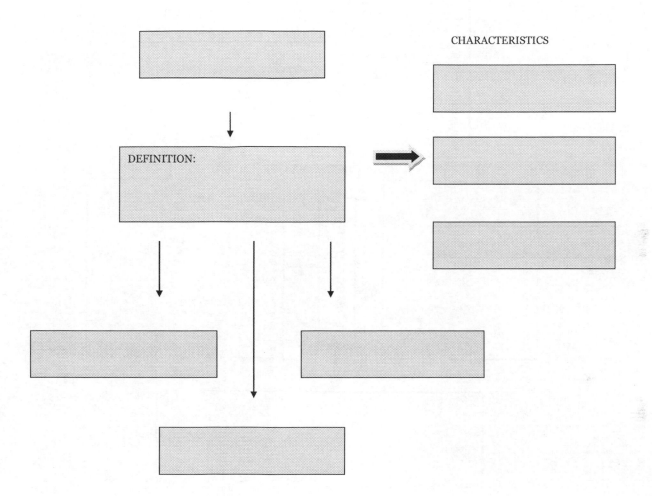

CHARACTERISTICS

DEFINITION:

EXAMPLES

15

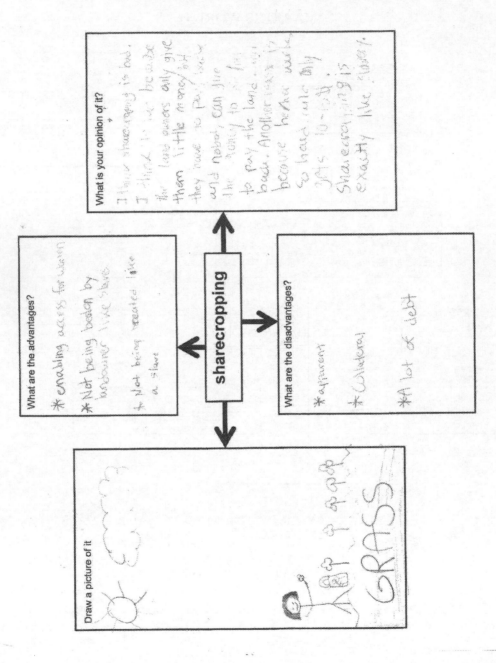

What is your opinion of it?

I think sharecropping is bad. I think it is so because the land owners only give them little money so they have to pay back and never can give the money to buy the land... I [?] bad. Another issue because I have wile to had [?] this to-day. Sharecropping is exactly like slavery.

What are the advantages?

* enabling access for tenant

* Not being beaten by landowners like slave

* Not being treated like a slave

sharecropping

What are the disadvantages?

* [?]

* children

* A lot of debt

Draw a picture of it

GRASS

16

STRATEGY 5

Don't Bug Me Vocabulary

Don't bug me vocabulary is very similar to the connection card but is intended for the elementary student. Students put important information about the vocabulary word on different parts of the bug.

<u>Suggested Use</u>:

The word is placed at the top of the bug. Students are to find the definition, an antonym, synonym, part of speech, and write a sentence. "Don't bug me" is a great pre-reading activity that allows students to use a dictionary and thesaurus and become familiar with finding words.

18

STRATEGY 6

Word Sets

Word sets are useful when trying to get students to make associations among words or concepts. This activity can be done in multiple ways.

<u>Suggested Use</u>:

The first way to use word sets is effective when used with an Active Board or Smart board. Different categories should be established at the top of the set. Below these categories can be pictures or words. Students are to classify the words or pictures into their correct categories.

The second type of word set involves giving students an established list of words. They can then identify the word that does not belong in the group of words or fill in the blank with the missing word.

Word Set Example #1

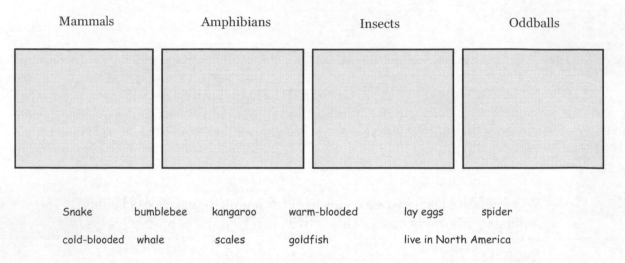

| Mammals | Amphibians | Insects | Oddballs |

Snake   bumblebee   kangaroo   warm-blooded   lay eggs   spider

cold-blooded   whale   scales   goldfish   live in North America

Word Set Example 2: Fill in the Blank Word Sets

Forms of Precipitation:

Rain

Hail

Snow

_____

Word Set Example 3: Identify the different word

pulley

inclined plane

telephone

lever

Confederate

Robert E. Lee

Abraham Lincoln

rebels

volcano

hurricane

tsunami

canyon

STRATEGY 7

Magic Words

The main purpose of magic words is to reinforce and extend the student's contextual knowledge of content area terms. This is a vocabulary activity of matching terms with definitions with a special arrangement of numbers. These numbers, when added across or down, always equal the same number. The sample on the next page has as its magic number-15.

<u>Suggested Use:</u>

This activity is a great way to reinforce new words in text. Students will have the opportunity to learn the words and their definitions. Each time the students match a word with its meaning (listed a-i in the sample list on the next page), they will write the number in the appropriate magic square grid. After all the squares are completed, they should add up the three numbers in each row and column to see if they are coming up with the magic number. This activity provides great opportunities for small group interaction and is a new twist on mundane matching exercises.

A 7	B 3	C 5	15
D 2	E 4	F 9	15
G 6	H 8	I 1	15
15	15	15	

A. Frog	1. Comes from a pupa/beautiful colors
B. Deer	2. Meows/house pet
C. Rabbit	3. Bambi was one
D. Cat	4. Barks/house pet
E. Dog	5. Hops/has floppy ears
F. Giraffe	6. Has gills/swims in water
G. Fish	7. Begins as tadpole/croaks
H. Elephant	8. Large animal/grey in color/big ears
I. Butterfly	9. Tall animal/long neck

23

STRATEGY 8

Splash

Using a word splash can be an effective way to see how much prior knowledge students have on a given topic. Creating a Word Splash is a very simple yet effective pre-reading strategy. Students are basically brainstorming all of the information that they know about a particular subject or topic.

<u>Suggested Use</u>:

This strategy should be teacher directed. The topic should be introduced to the class on the splash. Students should then have a brief discussion in small groups to come up with words about the topic. After the small groups work together, each group will contribute words or phrases to the class splash.

The teacher should make sure to discuss the words and phrases and their relationship to the topic. The discussion at this point will be more student-centered than teacher centered. The teacher should evaluate how much prior knowledge the class as a whole has on the topic. If students are struggling with ideas to put on the Word Splash, the teacher knows that a few minutes will be needed to increase background knowledge that is necessary to read the passage.

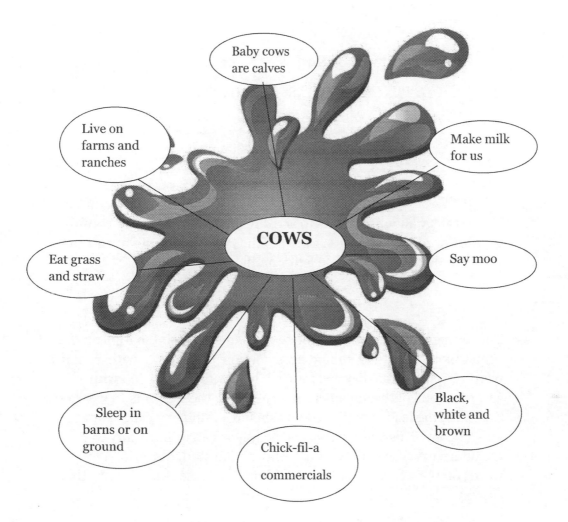

Baby cows are calves

Live on farms and ranches

Make milk for us

Eat grass and straw

COWS

Say moo

Sleep in barns or on ground

Chick-fil-a commercials

Black, white and brown

25

STRATEGY 9

Alphabet of Knowledge

This strategy allows students to activate prior knowledge by coming up with words and phrases related to the topic. Students record these words under the appropriate letter on the chart.

Suggested Use:

The teacher should give each student a handout with the topic in the center block. Students should be given time to come up with as many words or phrases as they can for each box, which is labeled with several letters of the alphabet. After allowing the students to work on the chart, the teacher and students should complete a classroom master copy. This activity can also be used as an opportunity to introduce new vocabulary words. Having the students write new words on their chart after learning about the topic could extend this activity.

The sample that follows is for the topic mammals. Students would contribute any words or phrases that relate to this topic. Under "ABC" they may put a word like "cats," and under "GHI," "have fur." Students should be encouraged to put at least one or two items in each column.

ALPHABET OF KNOWLEDGE

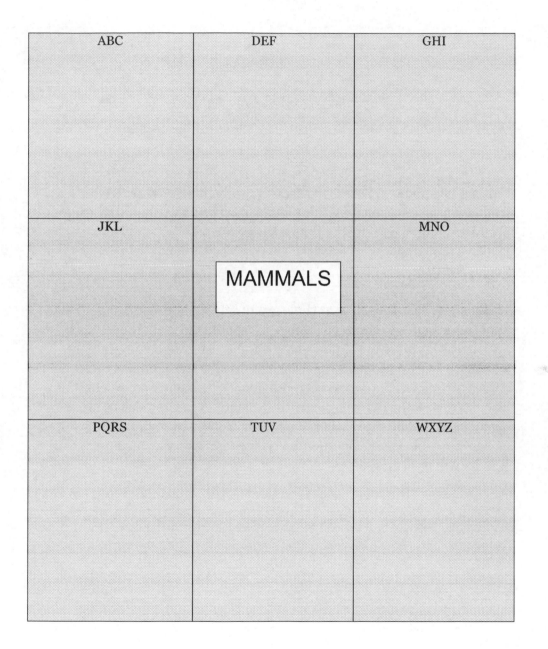

ABC	DEF	GHI
JKL	MAMMALS	MNO
PQRS	TUV	WXYZ

STRATEGY 10

Use Your Senses

This activity allows teachers to assess how much prior knowledge students have on a given topic. Students use their five senses to brainstorm information about the topic given.

<u>Suggested Use:</u>

This activity can be used as a whole group introduction and should take about 10 minutes to complete. Students should close their eyes and visualize everything they know about a topic. They will complete the worksheet, writing something in each of the five sense circles. After students complete the worksheet individually, the teacher should then discuss/review the information with students. A master class sense chart can be recorded by the teacher. For students that have limited background knowledge on the subject, the discussion at the end of this activity will be critical.

Use Your Senses

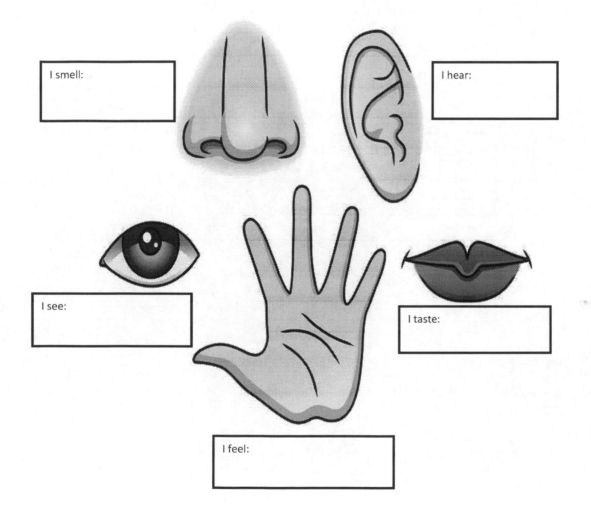

I smell:

I hear:

I see:

I taste:

I feel:

LET'S USE OUR SENSES

We have just finished Chapter 3 of our novel. As we move on to Chapter 4, close your eyes and imagine everything we have talked about so far. Now put what you expect to see, hear, feel, smell, and taste as we continue reading.

I see : I see a cot, a flor, a wall, and little lights

I hear: The night animals moving and trees moving.

I feel: The cot, the warmth and cold ness

I smell: food, wood, nature

I taste: food and water

STRATEGY **11**

KWL

The original KWL Chart has been used in all content areas to help students record what they KNOW about a topic, what they WANT TO KNOW about that topic (both the K and W are pre-reading portions of the chart), and what they have LEARNED after reading. Because students become quickly immune to the same chart format, a KWL made in a unique topic-related shape is a welcome change.

<u>Suggested Use:</u>

The KWL should be original to the material studied. Students should complete the first two parts of the chart before they begin reading the material. A master class KWL should be recorded by the teacher. After reading, it is imperative that students fill in the final part and discuss with the teacher.

KWL CHART FOR UNIT ON THE SOLAR SYSTEM

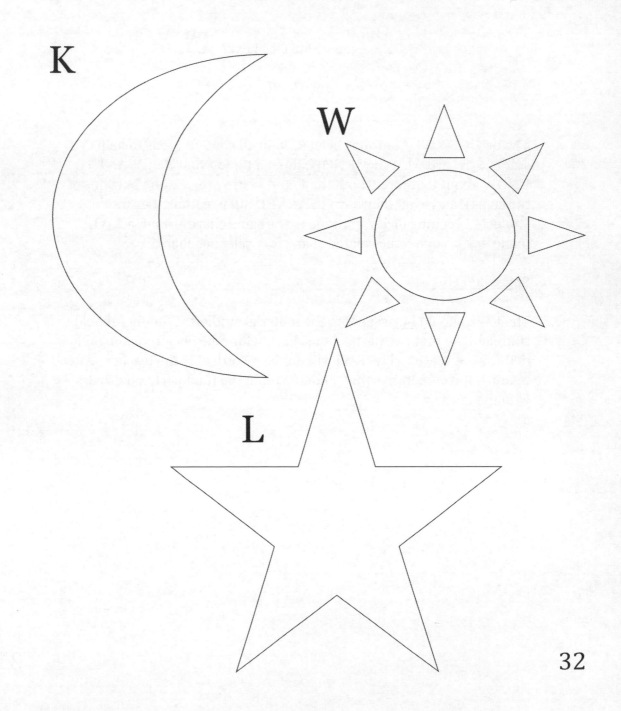

K

W

L

Louis Armstrong

Born in lousiana, new orleans 1901 Agust 4th
he was a jazz player, A musician

What songs did he write?
how did he died?

did he fins on school?
What was his nickname

Reaidied to nd
Am
Strong

I learned that he was a clarinet
Player and had ied because
he had a hear attack in his sleep
 he had to get raised by two jewish
Parent and leave Schoolin 5th grade and get A Job.

STRATEGY 12

Pique their Curiosity

This pre-reading strategy can be used in all content areas to create interest and curiosity in the topic that will be studied. This activity creates excitement among students and increases their interest in reading the material.

<u>Suggested Use:</u>

This strategy is most effective when used with a power point or the active board. The teacher should reveal clues one at a time. Students use these clues to predict what the reading passage is going to be about. The teacher should lead a discussion and give the students the opportunity to share their thoughts with other students. The class can then have a few possible consensus predictions.

Another way to use this strategy is to give students a handout with the clues listed. Students would then make their predictions individually before a class discussion.

Sample From Language Arts

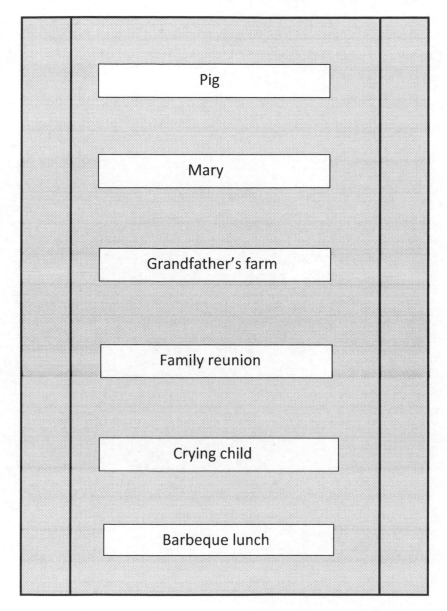

Story/Content Impression

Title: _____

Clues:

My Guess:

STRATEGY 13

I Predict

"I Predict" is an activity that allows students to make predictions prior to reading. "I Predict" contains two different prediction bubbles: in the first bubble, students write predictions about the passage to be read. After reading the passage, students use the second bubble to record if their predictions were true or false. They will then revise their false predictions to make them true statements.

<u>Suggested Use:</u>

This strategy can be completed individually or in small groups. However, it is essential that the teacher discuss predictions both prior to reading and after reading. This step should be completed as a whole group activity.

I Predict.....

Make at least five predictions about the story. After reading the passage, write a short statement explaining if your prediction was true or false. If your prediction statement was false, make a correction that will make the statement true.

My Predictions   Correct?

Scan the main parts of our chapter that we are about to read. Then I want you to make a prediction about whether we are going to be studying about jeans or genes. Put your prediction on the left pant leg. After we discuss our chapter, we will go back and put our conclusions on the right pant leg.

I predict that:
it is going to be about how cells grow and what happens. Also how cells inherir from one person to another.

I conclude that:
I was right about the cells growing new cells grow when old cells die. Also it tells how chicd starts as a single cell any grows. Also I was right about inheiring 23 chromosomes from each person forms you!

STRATEGY 14

Anticipation

Anticipation is used before reading to activate students' prior knowledge and build curiosity about a new topic. Before reading, students listen to or read several statements about key concepts presented in the text; they are often structured as a series of statements with which the students can choose to agree or disagree.

Suggested Use:
This activity works best when students complete the guide individually. Give students five to ten minutes to complete their Anticipation Guide. After everyone has completed the guide, discuss as a class. Have students give a "thumbs up" if they agree, or "thumbs down" if they disagree. The teacher should tally the results on the board so that students can look back after reading.

Anticipation

What do you think?	Yes 👍	No 👎
Egyptians were the first people to mummify their dead.		
Animals were also mummified in ancient Egypt.		
It only took about two hours to prepare a mummy for burial.		
Many of the kings and queens were buried with all of their treasure.		

QUESTION	DISAGREE	AGREE
Georgia was founded as a safe place for Quakers and Catholics to live.	X	
New England Colonies have extremely cold winters.		X
Philadelphia and New York City were the two biggest cities in the Mid-Atlantic Colonies.		X
People in the Southern Colonies lived close together, were very religious, and attended schools.	X	
The main industry for the New England Colonies was agriculture like rice, tobacco, and cotton.	X	

Predict-o-graph

A Predict-o-graph can be used to activate a student's background and vocabulary knowledge before reading a piece of text. This activity can be very beneficial for students because it provides a graphic organizer that they can use as they are introduced to important words in the passage they are about to read. This activity can be used during reading as well. While reading, students can correct their graphs if their predictions were not accurate.

Suggested Use:

The teacher gives students words from the text and a chart with categories. The students then put the words into the categories, making predictions about how the terms will be used in the reading. After the students complete the text, they should go back and correct any of their predictions that were wrong.

Predict-o-graph

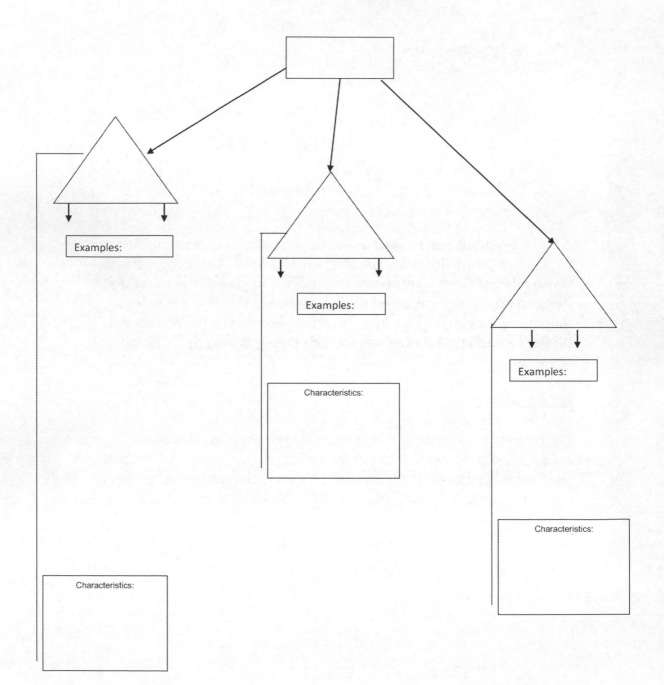

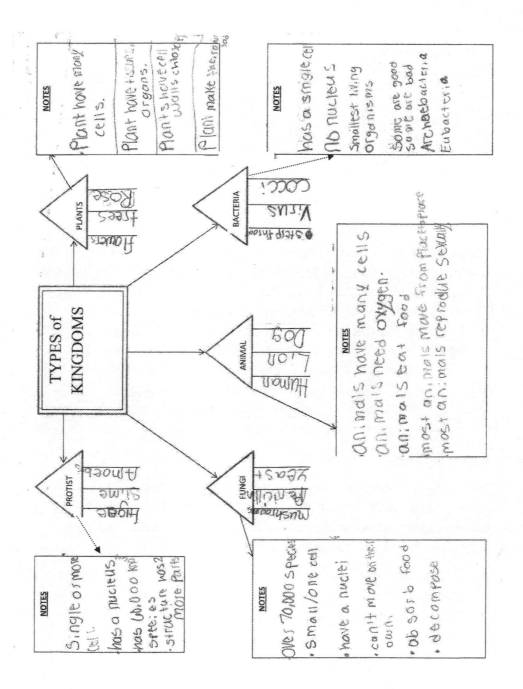

NOTES
- Plant have many cells.
- Plant have tissue + organs.
- Plants have cell walls + chlorophyll
- Plant make there own food

NOTES
- has a single cell
- No nucleus
- Smallest living organisms
- Some are good sort of or bad
- Archaebacteria, Eubacteria

PLANTS
Trees
Rose
Flowers

BACTERIA
Virus
cocci
Strep throat

TYPES of KINGDOMS

ANIMAL
Human
Lion
Dog

NOTES
animals have many cells
animals need oxygen.
animals eat food
most animals move from place to place
most animals reproduce sexually

PROTIST
Algae
Slime
Amoeba

FUNGI
mushroom
Panicillin
yeast

NOTES
- Single or more cell.
- has a nucleus
- has 60,000 kinds
- sreies
- structure was more parts

NOTES
- Over 70,000 species
- Small/one cell
- have a nuclei
- can't move on their own.
- absorb food
- decompose

45

STRATEGY 16

The Wondering Cube

The Wondering Cube can be used for a pre-reading strategy or an after-reading strategy. The cube is made using the template in this handbook. On each side of the cube, the teacher should write a question to activate prior knowledge. After introducing the topic, students could work in small groups and roll the cube to each other. After rolling the cube, students must answer the question on which the cube lands. These questions should be designed to lead the students into a discussion about the topic. After giving the students time to answer all six questions, the teacher should review the questions with the students to make sure every student understands.

Suggested Use:

This activity would be a great review activity about a topic that was discussed the day before. Using this cube, the teacher can check for understanding to determine if students have the prior knowledge needed to complete that day's activity.

An alternate use of this strategy is a larger cube that the teacher pre-loads with questions. The cube is then used as a group activity: the cube is rolled, questions are asked, and responses and discussion follow.

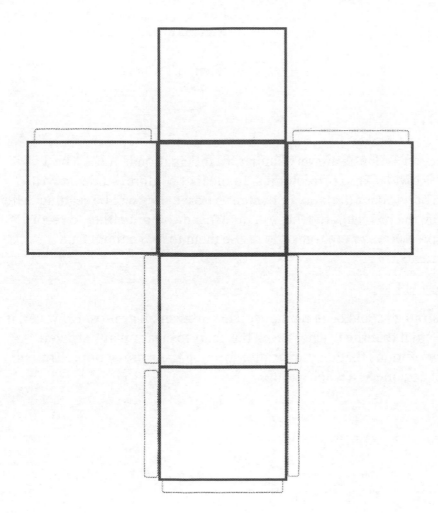

47

STRATEGY **17**

Prediction T-Chart

Prediction T-Charts are very similar to Anticipation Guides. The T – chart is divided into two columns. In the first column, students write predictions about the story or content passage they will be reading. After reading the passage, students use the second column either to record if their predictions were true or to revise them to make them true statements.

<u>Suggested Use:</u>

This strategy could be done individually or in small groups. However, it is essential that the teacher check the chart to clear up any student misconceptions that may arise after forming their predictions. This step would be done as a whole group.

T chart

Directions: Before reading the passage, write AT LEAST FIVE predictions about the story. After reading the passage, write a short statement explaining if your prediction was true or false. If your prediction statement was false, write a sentence that would make statement true.

BEFORE READING PREDICTIONS	TRUE/REVISED PREDICTIONS
1.	
2.	
3.	
4.	
5.	

STRATEGY **18**

My Best Guess

This pre-reading strategy is used to activate the student's prior knowledge prior to reading a story in language arts or a passage in another content area. Similar to a picture walk, the activity requires students to take a look at the title, pictures, and illustrations and record their responses on the worksheet.

<u>Suggested Use:</u>

Students should complete the activity individually prior to group discussion. The teacher should then lead a discussion, allowing students to share their "guesses" about the material that will be read.

My Best Guess

	Title of Story or Chapter:
Read the title. What do you think the story or chapter will be about?	
After flipping through the pages, what can you learn about the setting?	
After flipping through the pages, what can you learn about the characters?	
After flipping through the pages, what can you learn about the plot or conflict?	
Explain what you think of when you scan this book or chapter. Does it remind you of something else you have read?	

ESTIMATING AND MULTIPLYING NUMBERS WITH DECIMALS

MY BEST GUESS

QUESTIONS	ANSWERS
1. Have you multiplied decimals before?	I have but it confused me at first
2. Where would you use estimation of decimals in real life?	Maybe At stores when you need to count money, or at home when your collecting it
3. How do you think you would check for reasonableness when estimating whole numbers with decimals?	Put the two numbers together and if the decimal is close to the whole number then there you have your answer
4. What do you think 'ANNEX A ZERO' means??	When a zero is multiplied by a negative number
5. Would repeated addition or multiplication be easier when estimating whole numbers with decimals?	yes because when you multiply it then get the real number then see if the Are close then you have your answer

During Reading Strategies

STRATEGY **1**

Read it Together

"Read it Together" is a great process to use to ensure comprehension during whole group reading. This procedure is effective because it can be used to break long passages down into manageable parts for better comprehension.

<u>Suggested Use:</u>

1. Activate prior knowledge and discuss new vocabulary.
2. Ask students to read a selection of text silently (give students two or three minutes).
3. Instruct students to turn over their textbooks.
4. Ask the students to tell what they remember. (The teacher should write this information on the board or on a chart to give students a visual).
5. Discuss any inconsistencies.
6. Students can now use the book to correct any misconceptions they may have and to add more information.
7. Repeat steps 2-6 again. Continue this process until the entire passage has been covered.
8. Group students' information together using a semantic map.

54

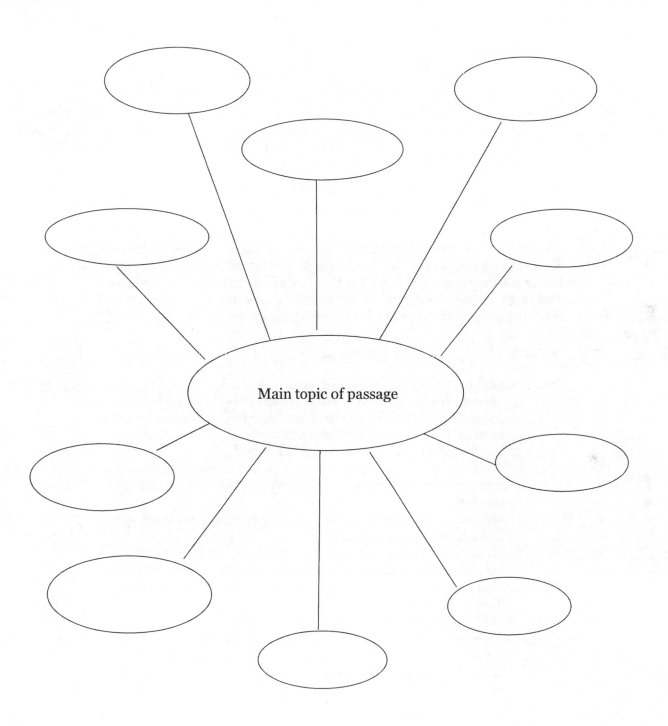

STRATEGY 2

Pyramid Puzzle

This method is designed to break long passages up into small segments. Students are not responsible for reading every word in the text. However, they are responsible for the part of the text they are assigned. The students become experts over their assigned material and then will relay the information to their other home group members.

Suggested Use:

Divide students into 4 person home groups.

1. Appoint one student from each group as the leader. (When doing this method for the first time, the leader should be the most mature person of the group.)
2. Divide the day's lesson into four segments.
3. Assign each student to learn one segment. Students should have direct access only to the information needed for learning their segment.
4. Students should be given enough time to read over their section and become familiar with it.
5. Students will then be divided into "temporary expert groups" by having one student from each home group join other students assigned to the same segment. Students should be given time to discuss the main points of their segment. They will write important facts on their puzzle pieces.
6. Students will return to their home groups. Each student will present his or her puzzle piece to the other group members to make the complete pyramid.

Sample Puzzle Piece:

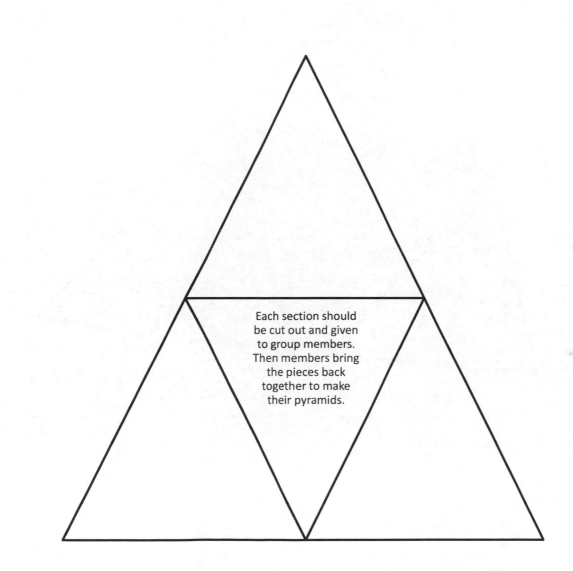

Each section should
be cut out and given
to group members.
Then members bring
the pieces back
together to make
their pyramids.

Columbus did not have maps to find the new land his crew wanted to go home

Ponce de Leon He fought with Native Ameri...

He had written off... maps to guide him on... the new land. He didn't have... John Cabot found...

Henry His voyage was blocked by Ice. His crew could not handle the cold climate.

STRATEGY 3

Double Entry Reading Journal

The Double Entry Reading Journal is designed to help students comprehend the information when the teacher is not readily available or when independent reading is assigned. These journal entries are meant to be meaningful and personal to each student. There is not a correct or incorrect journal entry.

Suggested Use:

These journals are designed by dividing a piece of paper into two parts. In the first column, students are to write their responses to what they learned. This is the space where students should write interesting facts, draw a picture of the main facts, or make comments about the selection. The other half of the paper is dedicated to information they learned while reading.

Double Entry Reading Journal

Comments about what you learned	What did you learn?

Double entry Journal

Info learned	Personal reflection
def, of Perpetul motion machine- energy that runs forever and shares extra energy,	It would be a great idea, nothing would run out of energy.
If you roll a ball across as smooth floor, you're watching a law of motion	It's cool because if there were no friction, It would not stop.
Sir Isaac Newton made a water powered clock.	The water dripped almost every minute.
Gravity pulls everything	If not, we would be in space.

Facts	Pictures
1 In 1497 John Cabot's explorations	that's a really long time ago
2 John perpares to sail across the Atlantic ocean in 1497	
3 He reached Canda he thought it was Asia.	
4 He explored the land and found no People and no silk + spices	
5 He sailed back to England and told the people.	

STRATEGY 4

Comprehension Monitoring Guide

A Comprehension Monitoring Guide is a helpful strategy to use during independent reading of a text. This activity gives students a guide or roadmap for their reading.

<u>Suggested Use:</u>
To use a comprehension monitoring guide, teachers should give each student one guide to complete individually while he is reading the passage. Typically the guide will be a list of agree/disagree or true/false statements. It is the student's job to read the passage carefully in order to answer the questions correctly. If a statement is false, the student must circle false and find the correct answer. If the statement is true, the student will simply circle true and move to the next question. Depending on the length of the passage, the teacher can include the page number on which the answer can be found; this would be beneficial for longer passages.

Comprehension Monitoring Guide

Statement from text	Agree? Disagree?		Correction

Name_____   Date 11-12-13

Comprehension Monitoring Guide

Directions: Answer the follow questions the best that you based off what you've already read.

True/False	1. Before Sequoyah, Cherokee language did not have an alphabet.
True/False	2. Sequoyah called the paper that the English wrote on "the talking trees".
True/False	3. Sequoyah did not have to study his language.
True/False	4. The word "Cherokee" is written the same in Sequoyah.
True/False	5. Ah-yoka lived with her father in a cabin, then it was burned.

65

STRATEGY 5
Read Along Guide

A Read Along Guide is designed to help students as they read independently. The statements in the guide should be placed in the order that they appear in the passage. This strategy helps ensure students understand the main points from the passage. In addition, the guide can later be used as a study guide.

Suggested Use:

The teacher will give each student a copy of the read along guide to use. Students should be encouraged to read carefully and answer the questions as they read. Teachers need to make sure to review the answers to this guide before moving on. Students need to make sure their answers are correct before using it later as a study guide.

Solar System Read Along Guide

1. Our solar system is approximately _____ years old.

2. List the planets that make up our solar system.
   1.   5.
   2.   6.
   3.   7.
   4.   8.

3. What planets were discovered after the telescope was introduced to the world?

4. There are _____ known moons in our solar system.

5. It was thought Saturn was the only planet with rings. We know now this is not true. What other planets have rings?

6. Most planets have their own magnetic field. The sun's magnetic field is called the _____.

7. It was first believe that the Earth was the center of the universe, and everything in the solar system orbited around the Earth. Who discovered this was not true? And what does Earth and the other planets and stars orbit around?

8. Most asteroids orbit between these two planets _____ and _____.

9. Earth's atmosphere is primary made up of _____ and _____.

STRATEGY **6**

RAM

RAM is designed to help students comprehend and remember what they have read. The acronym stands for:

    R- Read a paragraph or section of text
    A- Ask yourself – what is the main idea and two important details?
       List these on the graphic organizer.
    M- Move to the next section of the passage.

<u>Suggested Use:</u>

When introducing this strategy to your students, it is important to model each step. The teacher may wish to use this strategy as a whole class activity until students become comfortable with this process. Then students can use the strategy independently.

R   A   M

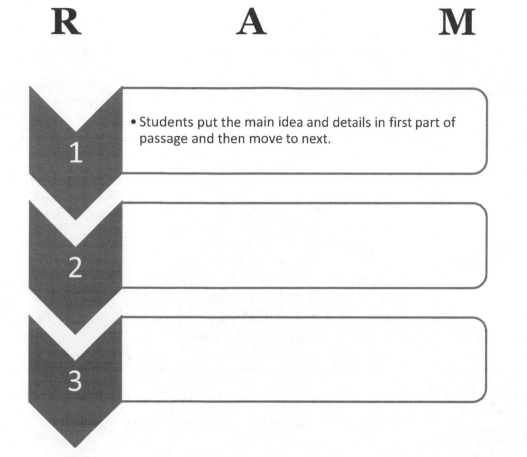

1
- Students put the main idea and details in first part of passage and then move to next.

2

3

R   A   M

R - Read a passage

A - Ask yourself—what is the main idea and two supporting details to support my main idea

M - Move to the next section of the passage and repeat the above steps

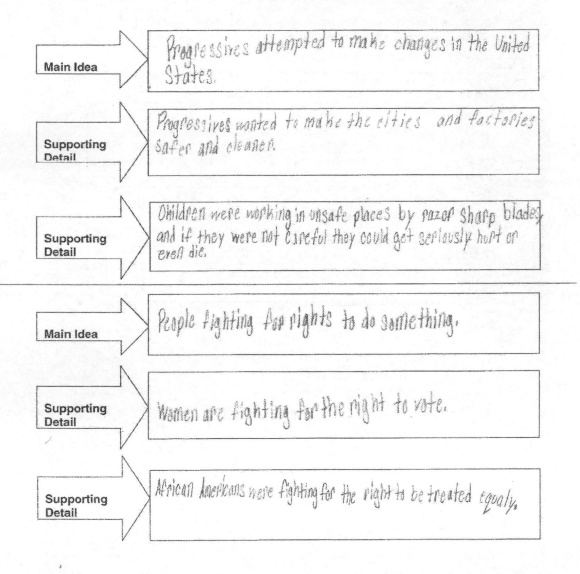

Main Idea
Progressives attempted to make changes in the United States.

Supporting Detail
Progressives wanted to make the cities and factories safer and cleaner.

Supporting Detail
Children were working in unsafe places by razor sharp blades, and if they were not careful they could get seriously hurt or even die.

Main Idea
People fighting for rights to do something.

Supporting Detail
Women are fighting for the right to vote.

Supporting Detail
African Americans were fighting for the right to be treated equally.

70

STRATEGY 7

The Main Event

This strategy is an effective way to teach students how to identify the main ideas in a passage. Students are given a worksheet with ten or more blank spaces. As students read the passage, they will write down the words or phrases that they believe are important to the passage. Students should also be able to give a brief explanation for why they chose that particular word.

Suggested Use:

This strategy is designed to be completed individually. However, after students identify their important words, students can pair up, compare their list of words, and discuss why they chose certain words. The teacher may also want to bring the class together as a whole and combine everyone's important words.

The Main Event

Find what you believe to be the ten most important words or phrases in our reading passage. List them on the left side of the chart. On the right side list the reason you believe it to be one of the main words.

Word	Importance?

The Main Event:

Find what you believe to be the 10 most important words or phrases in our reading passage. List them on the left side of the chart. On the right side, list the reason you believe it to be one of the main words.

Word	Why is it important?
Saber	Will's dad owned the saber
Yankees	Most of Will's family got killed by them.
Buttons	Will had buttons from Milita uniforms.
Charlie Page	Will's brother who got shot.
Elizebeth Anne Page	Family history of Will.
Elenor Jeanne Page	Another ancestor.
When Johnny Comes Marching Home	A song to prouhe Will.
Confederacy	The South.
War	Fighting for freedom.

After Reading Strategies

STRATEGY 1

I Have-Who Has?

"I have-Who has?" is an after reading activity which helps students with comprehension skills and recall of information. Students enjoy this game because it is a fun and easy way to review.

<u>Suggested Use:</u>

To play this game, distribute one card to each student in the class. On these cards, the teacher should have questions related to the reading that they have just completed, as well as an answer. As you distribute the cards, encourage students to begin thinking about what the question for their card might be so that they are prepared to answer. When all cards are distributed, select one student to go first. The play continues until the game comes back to the original card. That student answers and then says "stop" to signal the end of the game.

For example, the first card in a math review version of this game might read, "Who has 4 x 5?" The student whose card reads, "I have 20. Who has 6 x 7?" would then read his card. The game would continue until all cards have been used.

"I have - who has?"

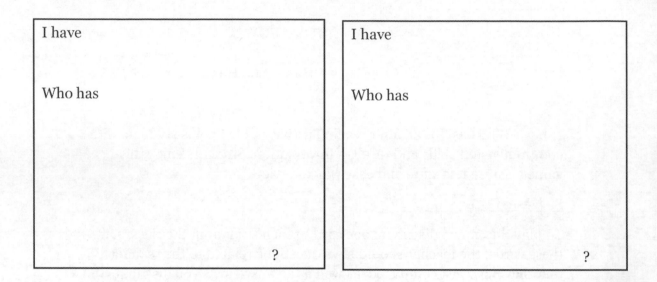

I have

Who has

?

I have

Who has

?

I have

Who has

?

I have

Who has

?

76

STRATEGY **2**

Comic Strip

The comic strip activity allows students to describe visually what happens in a story or a reading selection. Students make a personal connection to the reading passage by drawing and writing about what they have comprehended.

Suggested Use:

Have students fold a piece of paper like an accordion 2-3 times to make the boxes, or use the handout provided. This activity is meant to be done individually. Students should be given 15-20 minutes to create their comic strip. After students have completed their comic strips, the teacher would then lead a classroom presentation of the comic strips for those that want to share. During this activity, while students are creating their comic strips, the teacher should create one as well. The teacher should share her work as well.

Comic Strip Template

(Pictures)   (What happens first, next, third, and last)

Adjective Comic Strip

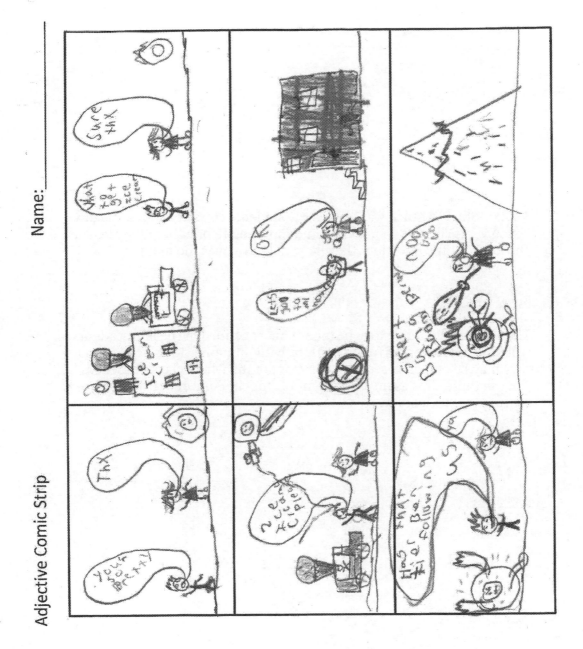

STRATEGY 3

The Exit Slip

An Exit Slip is a quick way to see how students comprehended the day's lesson. This slip of paper allows students to state one thing they learned and address any questions they may still have over the material presented.

Suggested Use:

The teacher should give each student an exit slip. On the slip students will be given the opportunity (with or without name) to ask questions they may be embarrassed to ask in front of the whole class. Teachers can use these slips as an assessment of student comprehension before moving on the next day.

My Exit Slip

One thing I learned today:_____

One question I still have:_____

I would like to know more about:_____

Sample of Exit Slip

What I learned today:

I learn that decimals
have so many numbers
in just in one place value

What I still have a question about:

when are we
going do percent %?

Name:

STRATEGY 4

Discussion Web

Discussion Webs are used to help students engage with and express their opinions about the text. Students are able to voice their opinions about a particular question that the teacher wishes to discuss.

<u>Suggested Use:</u>

Students should first be given an individual sheet on which to work. Students will list their reasons for the opinions that they have. Then the activity becomes a whole class activity. The teacher should lead a discussion with a "master" discussion web, listing the reasons that students give on both sides of the topic. A class consensus can be reached after discussion of both sides of the issue.

Discussion Web

QUESTION:

_____

_____

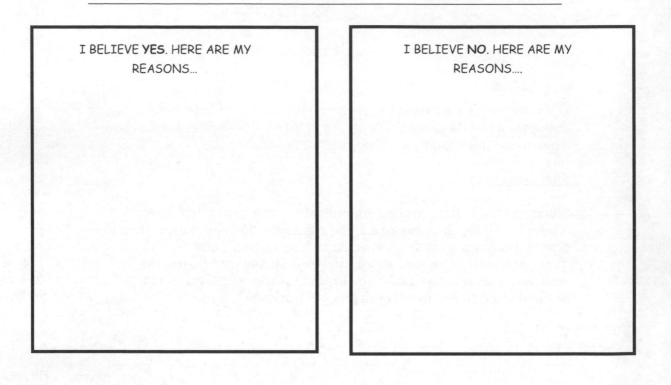

I BELIEVE **YES**. HERE ARE MY REASONS...

I BELIEVE **NO**. HERE ARE MY REASONS....

SUMMARY: _____ NUMBER STUDENTS BELIEVE YES.
         _____ NUMBER STUDENTS BELIEVE NO.

The majority of our class believes:

Math Discussion Web

When multiplying decimals, the placement of a decimal in the product is not important.

true
Yes

false
No

Reasons	Reasons
	• If you put the decimal in the wrong place your whole answer is wrong. 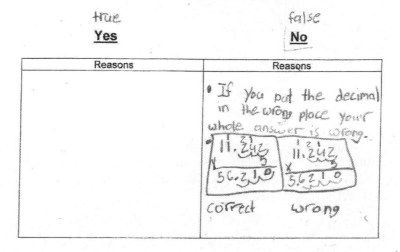 correct wrong

<u>**Summary:**</u>
The correct one is bigger and right because of the decimal. The wrong one is smaller because of the decimal. So The decimal means alot.

85

STRATEGY 5

Cloze Passage

A Cloze Passage is an effective way to review a selection from the text. This activity takes the main ideas from a text and pulls them together into a paragraph. The student goes through the passage and fills in the missing words.

<u>Suggested Use:</u>

For younger students, a word bank should be included with every passage. To make the passage more challenging, the teacher could add more words in the bank than needed. Each student should complete a cloze passage individually. After giving the students time to complete their passages, the teacher should review the cloze passage with the entire class.

Cloze Passage

All the stages in the life of an animal make up the animal's

_____ _____. A butterfly goes through _____

stages. During the first stage the butterfly lays _____. The second

stage occurs when a _____ hatches from the egg. This is also

called the _____ of the butterfly. During this stage, the future

butterfly eats all the time and grows and grows. The third stage occurs

when the larva forms a hard covering around itself called _____.

The fourth and final stage occurs when the case around the insect

breaks. Finally, a _____ will appear.

Word Bank		
Caterpillar	Eggs	Pupa
Butterfly	Larva	Life Cycle
Four	Spider	

STRATEGY 6

Quick Write/Sketch

Quick Write/Sketch is an activity that allows students to summarize what they have read. Many students struggle with summarizing, and this strategy allows them to practice this important skill.

Suggested Use:

This worksheet gives students a space to write a brief summary and a space to draw a picture. At the bottom of the worksheet is a section for new vocabulary words. Quick Write/Sketch should be completed individually. However, the teacher should take time to review the worksheet with the entire class.

Quick Write/Sketch

Quick Write	Quick Sketch

New Words I Learned...

Quick Write/Sketch

Quick Sketch

Quick Write

simple machines make
work alot easen for
everyone

New Words I Learned...

Falcram   Simple machine

STRATEGY 7

12 Question Review

This after reading strategy allows students to devise their own review questions for a story or a section of text. There are twelve blocks on the sheet for students to fill with what they consider the most important information in the passage. The teacher may adjust the number of blocks on the chart based on student grade level.

Suggested Use:

Students should first work individually on their twelve questions. Then students can be put in pairs or groups to "quiz" other classmates. As an added bonus, the teacher may announce that she will use some questions from the students' sheets for a future assessment.

12 Question Review

Put a review question in each square below. Some words you may wish to use to start your questions are: name, explain, compare, contrast, describe, tell, define, summarize, create, predict, conclude, organize, and evaluate.

6 Question Review:

Create 6 decimal problems. You may choose any of the following: comparing, addition, subtraction, decimal patterns, or multiplication.

657.32 × 15.12	500.709 +900.392	Put the numbers in order from greatest to least. 777.89 300.98 563.72
932.57 × 13.02	437.989 +721.432	Put the numbers in order from least to greatest. 20.37 998.378 200.489 567.963

STRATEGY **8**

Let's Solve the Problem

"Let's Solve the Problem" helps students identify the problem or conflict in a language arts story or a passage in social studies. After reading the text, the teacher and the students discuss the main conflict. Students will then come up with three possible solutions that can solve the problem. However, students are required to list pros and cons to each solution. After listing three possible solutions, students are to choose their best solution and defend why it is the best solution.

Suggested Use:

After group discussion of the problem or conflict in the story, the chart should be completed in a small group of two to three students. The students will have a discussion about the solutions and have to decide as a group the top three solutions. Students will then discuss the problem and possible solutions with the whole class.

Let's Solve the Problem

What is the problem?	

Whose problem is it? Why is it a problem?	

What are three possible solutions?	Pros and Cons for each solution
1.	(+) (-)
2.	(+) (-)
3.	(+) (-)

What is the best solution? And why?

STRATEGY 9

Trading Cards

After reading have students select their favorite character out of a story or a historical figure in another content area. Pass out a blank "trading card" to each student. On the trading cards, instruct students to draw a picture of the character, write the name of the character, explain why the character was important, and write a short summary about the character as well as why they like that particular person.

Suggested Use:
Give all students an opportunity to present their cards to the class. Have students pass their cards around to their peers so all students can see the class set of trading cards.

Sample Trading Card

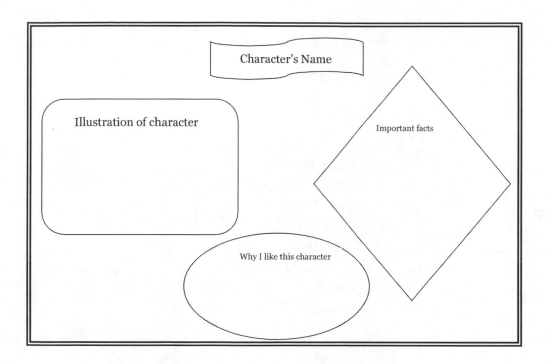

Sample Trading Cards from 5th grade: Other facts on back side of card

Robert E. Lee

Confederate General who led the South against the Union in the Civil War.

Abraham Lincoln

Abraham Lincoln was the president during the Civil War.

Thomas "Stonewall" Jackson

Confederate general under Robert E. Lee in the Civil War

Ulysses S. Grant

The Hero of the Civil War

STRATEGY **10**

3-2-1

The 3-2-1- activity is a simple way for students to show what they have learned or ask questions about a topic. This strategy gives students the opportunity to summarize some key ideas, rethink them in order to focus on those that they are most interested in, and then pose a question that can reveal questions they still have. This activity is especially helpful when given as a homework assignment in addition to reading.

<u>Suggested Use:</u>

This strategy involves students making a list of three things they discovered in their reading, two things they found interesting, and one question they still have. When students come to class with the completed sheets, the teacher can lead a discussion based on their responses and questions.

3 _____

_____

_____

2 _____

_____

1 _____

STRATEGY 11

Three in a Row

Three in a Row is an after reading activity that promotes comprehension skills, as well as allowing students to use their creativity. Students generally enjoy this activity, not only because it is in the form of a game, but because they will have the option of choosing which assignments they want to complete. This activity offers students multiple ways to provide evidence of their mastery of the material.

<u>Suggested Use:</u>

This activity is based on the "tic-tac-toe" game. The teacher should design a game board to review the particular topic that students have been studying. Students must complete assignments and place an X in the boxes in order to complete the activity- in a vertical, horizontal, or diagonal row. The center block is typically a given X, but the teacher may wish to substitute another assignment in that block so that students complete three activities.

Three in a Row

Make a large bubble map which outlines the main ideas we have discussed in this unit on the Civil War.	You are a reporter on the scene. Write a newspaper article about Lee's surrender to Grant.	You are an artist. Draw a picture of something of significance during the time period we have been studying.
Make a large poster-sized time line of the events we have discussed in our unit.	Free ⊠ space	Make a set of trading cards for at least five of the historical figures we have studied in this unit.
Using three sizes of sticky notes, summarize the main idea of the unit on the biggest note-then again on the medium size note- then again on the smaller note.	Pretend that you are a Union or Confederate soldier at the Battle of Gettysburg. Write a letter home to your parents or sweetheart, telling them of your situation.	You have been given the opportunity to interview President Lincoln. List your questions followed by the President's remarks.

STRATEGY **12**

Timelines

Timelines are effective to use with students who have just completed a reading passage, story, or novel. Timelines not only help readers identify important events, but they also can lead readers to make inferences about how one event relates to another or how one event inspired or lead to another.

Have students create their own timeline on a piece of paper, or the teacher can provide one with dates or specific information already supplied. After students have filled out their timelines, a larger class version can also be made.

Timeline Samples

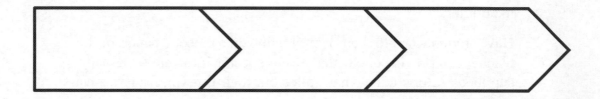

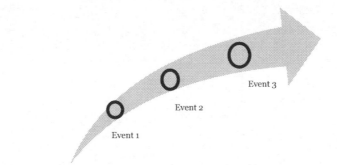

STRATEGY **13**

Character Map

Character maps can be used to help students remember important facts about fictional or historical characters. These maps help students keep character information organized.

<u>Suggested Use:</u>

To make a character map, have students write a character's name in the center of the chart and then use other boxes to represent character aspects: speech, thoughts, actions, and appearance, as well as what others (characters) think or say about the character. Other categories could include the character's feelings, talents, skills, and personality. For historical characters, categories could include obstacles faced, significant achievements, and special life events. The character map can be customized by the teacher for use in the classroom.

Character Map

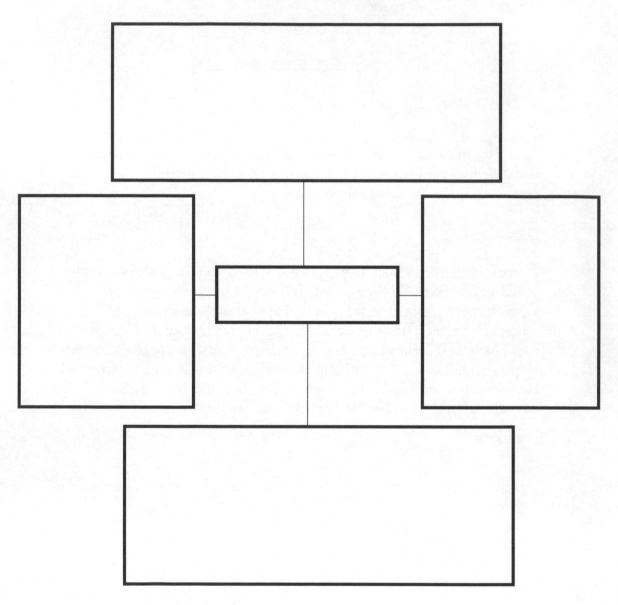

STRATEGY 14

Venn Diagrams

Venn Diagrams have been used for many years to encourage students to think about and discuss similarities and differences between two topics or characters. Venn diagrams help students organize their thoughts.

Traditional Venn diagrams have consisted of two or more circles that overlap. However, changing the form of the Venn diagram sparks student interest and makes the activity more interesting and meaningful for the student.

Suggested Use:

The teacher can construct a Venn diagram which carries out the theme of a story or text, while maintaining the areas for comparison and contrast. On the following page are two Venn diagrams: one is for a comparison/contrast of alligators and crocodiles, while the other is for lions and tigers. Large Venn diagrams can be laminated and used by the teacher with dry erase markers, while students should have a smaller diagram on which to work.

Unique Venn Diagrams

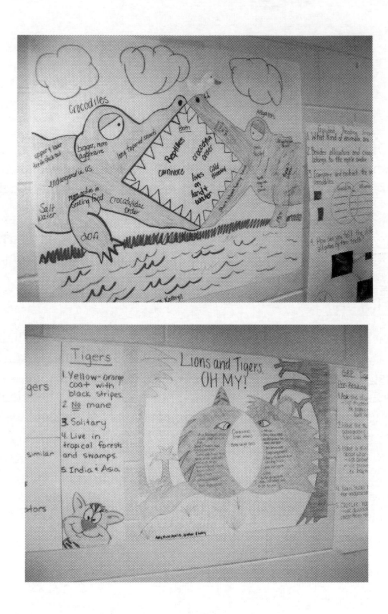

STRATEGY 15

Social Media Page

This after reading activity is based on a current social media outlet, Facebook. Students are given the opportunity to create a page based on a character in language arts or a historical figure.

<u>Suggested Use:</u>

The teacher should distribute one worksheet to each student. A completed sheet on a commonly known figure (for example, George Washington) can be shown to students so that they understand what they will be creating. Students will draw a picture of the character, list friends, hobbies, interests, and post two updates to the page.

Name	Friends	Inbox (3)	Home Page

Draw a picture of character or historical figure

Home Page	Photos	Info	+

Update status   **Add photo**

What's new with you?

Character's personal info

Post #1

_____
_____
_____
_____
_____
_____
_____

Friends

Post #2

_____
_____
_____
_____
_____
_____
_____

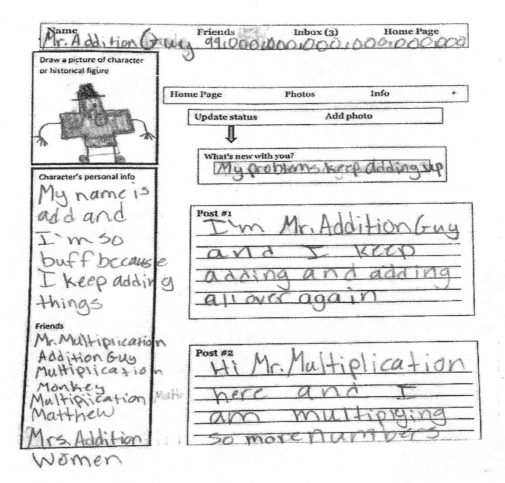

Name	Friends	Inbox (3)	Home Page

Mr. Addition Guy   99,000,000,000,000,000,000

Draw a picture of character or historical figure

Home Page	Photos	Info	+

Update status   **Add photo**

What's new with you?
My problems keep adding up

Character's personal info

My name is
add and
I'm so
buff because
I keep adding
things

Friends
Mr. Multiplication
Addition Guy
Multiplication
Monkey
Multiplication
Matthew
Mrs. Addition
Women

Post #1
I'm Mr. Addition Guy
and I keep
adding and adding
all over again

Post #2
Hi Mr. Multiplication
here and I
am multiplying
so more numbers

111

STRATEGY 16

Story Map

A story map is a visual depiction of the major literary elements in a story. The diagram enables students to map out these elements and see how they all fit and work together to tell the story.

Suggested Use:

Story maps are used to increase students' comprehension of selections by organizing and sequencing main story events. They also increase students' awareness that story characters and events are interrelated. After completing a story/book, give each student a copy of a story map to complete individually.

Story Map

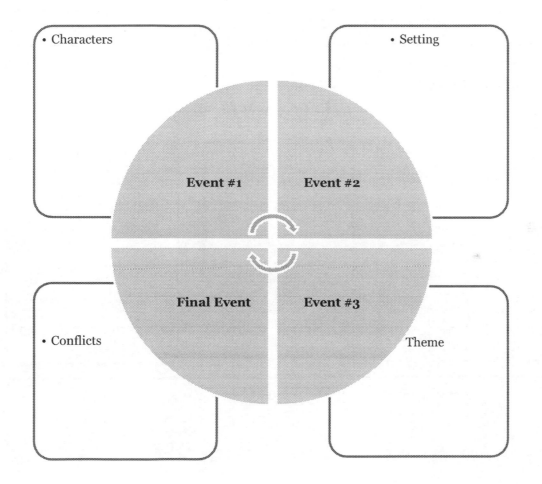

- Characters

- Setting

Event #1 Event #2

Final Event Event #3

- Conflicts

Theme

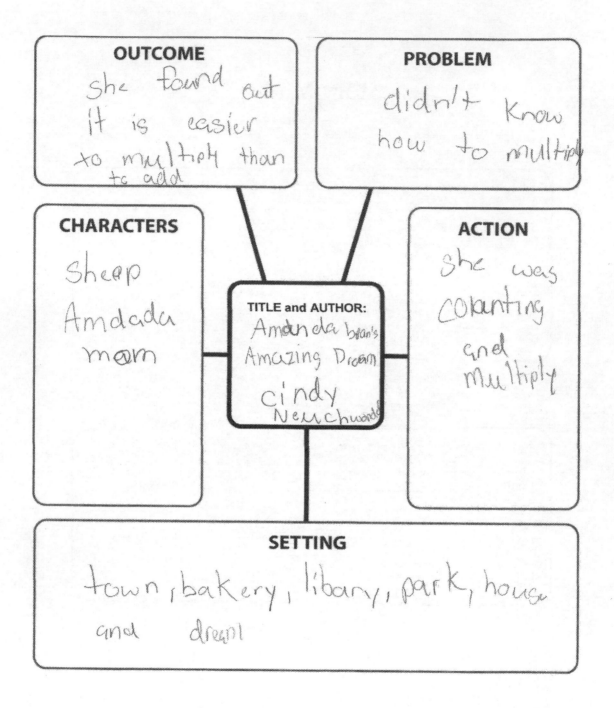

OUTCOME

she found out it is easier to multiply than to add

PROBLEM

didn't know how to multiply

CHARACTERS

Sheep
Amdada
mom

TITLE and AUTHOR:

Amanda bean's Amazing Dream

cindy Neuchwande

ACTION

she was counting and multiply

SETTING

town, bakery, libany, park, house and dream

114

STRATEGY 17

Comparison Chart

The comparison chart activity uses a grid to help students explore how sets of things are related to one another. By completing and analyzing the grid, students are able to see connections, make predictions, and master important concepts.

Suggested Use:

To use a comparison chart, the teacher will provide students with key words and important features related to the topic. The vocabulary words should be listed down the left hand column and the features of the topic across the top row of the chart. Teachers should have students place a "+" sign in the matrix when a word aligns with a particular feature of the topic. If the word does not align, students may put a "−" in the grid. If students are unable to determine a relationship they may leave it blank. For younger students, a smiley face can be used in place of the "+" sign.

115

Comparison Chart

Key words ⇩	Characteristics ⇒					

\+ for yes and − for no

☺ for yes and ☹ for no

STRATEGY 18

R.I.P.

This after reading activity is a creative way for students to summarize what they know about a historical or fictional character. Similar to an obituary, the R.I.P. tombstone serves as a more creative summary of a person's life and achievements.

<u>Suggested Use:</u>

Students should be given a tombstone template, along with instructions to create an appropriate epitaph for the character. A sample of completed R.I.P. tombstones for explorers appears on the next page.

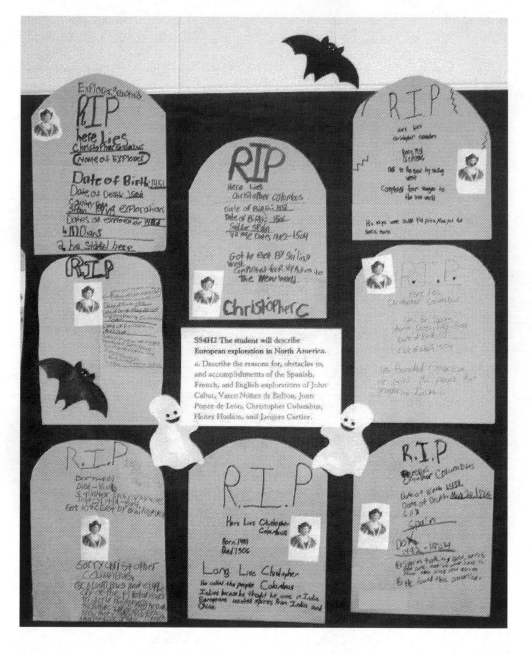

STRATEGY **19**

Historical News Stories/Ads

Because students are so bombarded with television news and advertising, they forget how information was spread by the written and printed word prior to the last half of the 20th century. At that time all news stories and advertising were in the form of newspaper articles, ads, posters, or flyers.

After studying about a particular time period in history, students can write a news story or create an advertisement for publication in a period newspaper.

Suggested Use:

Many examples of historic news stories/ads are available on the internet. Show several of these to students prior to assigning this activity.

Telegraph sends message to Lincoln in the White House.

After William Sherman fought against the Confederates in Atlanta, GA, he sent a telegraph (shown above) to Lincoln of his victory. He said, "Atlanta is ours, and fairly won."

London Times

April 1610-11

Henry Hudson's Final Voyage

Katherine Hudson asks the people and London Times for assistance. She is very worried about her husband Henry and son John. If anyone has heard anything or know where they might be, please contact the London Times.

Seems her husband Henry, son John and his crew left in April. They set sail from England on the ship the Discovery. Once again trying to find a new route to Asia. Captain Hudson's other 3 trips were not very successful. Henry did have a strait, river and a bay named after him.

After hearing her cry for help, I decided to investigate. My sources have told me that Henry and John were last seen boarding a small boat. His crew became angry with him and didn't trust his skills as a captain any longer. Low on supplies and trapped in ice the whole winter. There will be further examination into the crew's deeds.

Henry Hudson (English captain)

122

STRATEGY **20**

Please Join Us

This activity allows students to write an invitation to a particular event, as if the invitation were written by the actual people (in history or in a fictional story) who participated in or witnessed the events. Invitations in history often took the form of advertisements printed in newspapers or flyers to be posted in public places. Formal invitations were usually only sent for private parties or celebrations.

<u>Suggested Use:</u>

Show a sample of an invitation to a historical event. Tell students to concentrate on the time and occasion of the historical event, as well as the purpose or goal of the gathering.

Public Meeting

Come down to the
Martin Luther King JR.

I Have a dream speech.
It will be on August
28th 1963 in Woobbion DC.

((Sincerly))
MLKJ

124

Boston tea Party

No"Taxition
Without repersentation

Were - on the Ships by the habor

When - Dec. 16, 1773

Why - Colonist thought that British Should step the tax then for tea.

OBject - Dump all the tea in the harbor.

There will be a march through Town.

Join the Sons of liberty! Step the taxes Be free of taxes

Sincerly, Paul revere

125

STRATEGY **21**

Character Journals

Students should choose one important day in the life of a character or historical figure and record the events of the day in a personal journal. Not only does this activity assess student comprehension of the reading material, but it also provides an informal method of writing.

Suggested Use:

Each student should be given a journal page on which to record his thoughts. The teacher may wish to copy the template on "aged" paper, especially if the journal entry will be written from an earlier time period.

Today is

Dear Journal,

I woke up the day of the race exited but slightly scared. It was as if the whole race from lastyear kept replaying in my head, but I ignored it and got ready to go. My number was Six, which wasn't so bad. The dogs were great and ready to run, even when they got tangled by snow mobile! I was in lead for a very long time, so I had time to stop. I wanted to race, thanks to my great dogs.

After reading our story this week, select a character from the story and write a journal entry from that character's point of view. Include events, other characters, and any struggles or achievements the character went through, or feelings the character may have had in the story.